The basilica of the Sagrada Familia

The basilica of the Sagrada Familia is unique in the world. Besides its enormous dimensions, the importance of the temple stems from the absolute originality of its style, its revolutionary technical solutions and the mysticism which its brilliant creator, Antoni Gaudí imprinted on each one of the stones.

CONTENTS

A great temple is born

THE SAGRADA FAMILIA IS WELL-KNOWN THROUGHOUT THE WORLD, BUT IT ACTUALLY STARTED OUT AS A LOCAL PROJECT, CONCEIVED AND FINANCED BY A CHRISTIAN ASSOCIATION.

The emergence of the Sagrada Familia was fruit of a concrete social, political and cultural reality. In the last third of the 19th century, Catalan society kept an eye on what was changing in the world while at the same time was trying to recapture its identity as a people. This nationalist feeling was linked to a spiritual resurgence that spread through the lower to the upper classes; from the political class up to great figures in Catalan arts and literature. Within this context, Josep Maria Bocabella, President and Founder of the Association of Devotees to Saint Joseph, a religious group in Barcelona which by 1878 had already acquired 500,000 followers, decided to erect a temple funded by his own savings and donations from worshippers. Thus, the Sagrada Familia was born, a church made for and built by the people. On the 19th of March of 1882, its first stone was laid. In the Notarial Deed of the Ceremony its purpose was expressed: "Awake from tepidness those drowsy hearts. May Faith exult. Be charitable. Contribute so the Lord takes pity on the country..." What Bocabella couldn't imagine was to what extent this temple, which had been inspired by his faith in Saint Joseph, would eventually become one of the works of reference for architecture of all time. The shaper of this magnificent work was Antoni Gaudí, who would brilliantly transform this former neo-gothic style project into an absolutely unique temple.

THE PROMOTER
Josep Maria Bocabella
Driven by his devotion to Saint Joseph, José Maria Bocabella wanted to dedicate a temple to the Holy Family.

THE FIRST ARCHITECT
Francisco del Villar
This diocesan architect devised the initial project and was at the helm of building work on the Sagrada Familia until his resignation in 1883.

THE SECOND ARCHITECT
Antoni Gaudí
When he took charge of the Sagrada Familia project in 1883, Gaudí was a young architect with little work constructed, but was already well-known for his enormous energy and originality.

Gaudí becomes the temple's architect

After the resignation of the architect Francisco del Villar, the promoter Josep Maria Bocabella offered control of the building work to his technical adviser, Joan Martorell, who declined but proposed one of his collaborators, Antoni Gaudí, to lead the project. It was the year 1883 and Gaudí was a young architect who by the age of 31 had already demonstrated excellent abilities. Gaudí's genius rapidly went beyond the original project, transforming it into a universal masterpiece. Enthused about the project, Antoni Gaudí officially became the temple's architect on the third of November, 1883. At that time, construction on the crypt's pillars, designed by Del Villar, had already begun and one of the first things that Gaudí did, was to transform them, providing them with naturalistic capitals. In 1884, the first plans of Sagrada Familia to be signed by Gaudí were for the design of the Chapel of Saint Joseph, situated in the temple crypt. Its construction was rapid and mass was first held at its altar on the 19th of March, 1885. Nonetheless, the crypt wasn't finished until 1891, with a few of the chapels still remaining to be decorated.

In search of the perfect temple

In the commission of the temple of the Sagrada Familia, Antoni Gaudí took the opportunity to explore all of its architectonic potential and to achieve what no other architect had managed for centuries before him: the construction of the perfect temple. With this goal in mind, he concentrated all his efforts on ensuring that the whole of the temple would be in perfect consonance with his final mission, which was none other than the celebration of liturgical rites.

Construction of the temple crypt

The temple seen from Hospital Sant Pau

THE SAGRADA FAMILIA TEMPLE IN 1928. This photograph shows what the temple's surroundings were like in 1928. When work commenced, this area of the Eixample was far away from the centre and was a neighbourhood still in construction and inhabited by labourers. Nowadays it is a residential area in a hubbub of commercial activity.

He therefore drew on all of his innovative artistic and architectonic resources so that they could be perfectly adapted to the practice of religious cult. With the passing of the years and propelled by his anxiety for perfection, Gaudí gathered a sound religious knowledge along with a growing faith, converting him into an expert on liturgical themes. The architect envisaged the Sagrada Familia as a Bible made of stone, which told the history and mysteries of the Christian faith. On the exterior of the temple he represented the Church by means of apostles, evangelists, the Virgin and the saints. The cross, which tops the main tower, symbolizes the triumph of Jesus' church and the façades evoke three transcendental moments in Christ's lifetime: his birth (Nativity), death (Passion) and resurrection (Glory). The interior refers to the universal church and the crossing, to the Celestial Jerusalem, mystic symbol of peace. All in all, Gaudí managed to combine his faith and his artistic genius to transform the Sagrada Familia temple into a universal masterpiece.

The Passion façade

The crypt below the temple

GAUDÍ MANAGED TO ENDOW THE CRYPT WITH ITS OWN
PARTICULAR STYLE, IN SPITE OF NOT HAVING CARRIED OUT
GREAT CHANGES TO DEL VILLAR'S INITIAL PROJECT.

Excavation work on the crypt commenced between April and May in
1882, when the temple was still under the control of the diocesan architect Francisco del Villar. A few months later Del Villar resigned and
Gaudí took over the project. However, the architect from Reus had to ac-
cept what had already been built, given that to drastically change the original plan would have supposed investing a large sum of money, which was
completely out of the question considering that the temple was funded
with the worshippers' alms. Even so, Gaudí managed to introduce some
changes into the crypt which were more in keeping with his own architectural vision. Amongst his contributions stand out the construction of the
ditch and the raising of the columns. Likewise, he decided to decorate the
column capitals with naturalistic motifs, which the sculptor Llorenç
Matamala was commissioned to work on. Located below the apse, the
crypt is made up of seven apse chapels, in front of which are five others in
a straight line, a deambulatory and a central area of almost circular shape
measuring 40 metres long by 30 metres wide, over which the church pres-
bytery will be situated. To reach this area two winding staircases were built
and are situated on either side of the apse. These two stairs uniting the
temple in vertical form, permit the accessibility between different levels
and upper areas. Declared to be a World Heritage Site by UNESCO in the
year 2005, the temple crypt has been used as a parish church since 1930.

Stained glass window

Columns. Antoni Gaudí finished off the capitals with vegetable or naturalistic motifs.

Gaudí's first interventions

The crypt, which in Greek means hidden place, is a temple space which brings to mind the catacombs or subterranean places where the first Christians hid in times of persecution. Antoni Gaudí took control of the construction of the temple when the raising of the crypt's columns had already commenced. The former project, which was led by architect Francisco del Villar, was of pure neo-gothic style and Antoni Gaudí could only vary the elements which wouldn't affect the structure too much, such as raising the vault and adorning the capitals with naturalist details. He also surrounded the crypt with a deep ditch to prevent damp and, at the same time, to obtain illumination as well as direct and natural ventilation.

The interior layout of the crypt

The crypt is made up of seven chapels dedicated to the Holy Family of Jesus Christ which form a rotunda, in front of which are five other chapels in a straight line. Of these five chapels, the middle one houses the central altar, which is where mass is celebrated. According to what was originally planned, this central zone of the crypt will contain in the future, a reproduction of The Holy House of Nazareth, like the one venerated in Loreto.

Floor detail. Polychromatic mosaic depicting a bird feeding on a vine.

The Holy Family. Relief positioned on the central altar.

The crypt's chapels

The seven chapels which make up the semi-circle are dedicated to the Holy Family of Jesus. In the centre are the chapel of Saint Joseph, the Sacred Heart that represents Jesus' most human side, and that of the Immaculate Conception, dedicated to the Virgin Mary. Two other chapels are devoted to the Virgin's parents: Saint Joachim and Saint Anne. At one end, rises the Chapel of Saint John the Baptist, Jesus' cousin, and at the opposite far end, is the chapel dedicated to Saint Elisabeth, Mary's cousin and Saint John's mother, and to her spouse Saint Zachariah.

The ceiling: the vault system

The crypt is covered over by a series of vaults supported by numerous Gothic style arches and columns. Each vault has a keystone or central stone on which different elements are sculpted. Gaudí modified Villar's project in order that the central vault, finished off with a great keystone representing the Annunciation, would be higher than the chapels. With this difference in height, he managed to add some small windows which gave better illumination and ventilation to the central nave.

● **THE ANNUNCIATION OF MARY.** This polychromatic relief, a representation of the
● Annunciation by Flotats, was positioned by Gaudí at the point where the two large
● arches converge. Kneeling down with crossed arms, demonstrates her submission and
loyalty. Mary accepts the complex mission which God has in store for her.

● ● ●
THE KEYSTONES

The keystone of the deambulatory vault

The keystone of the chapel of Saint Joseph

The keystone of the chapel of Saint Anne

● ● ●
PHOTOGRAPHS

❶ **Central altar.** ❷ **Virgin of Montserrat.** ❸ **Chapel of Our Lady Carmen.** Gaudí wanted to be buried at the feet of this Virgin, to whom he was very devoted. His tombstone reads: *Antonius Gaudí Cornet, reusensis.* ❹ **The sacristy door.**

The apse and the cloister

IN CONSONANCE WITH HIS ERA, ANTONI GAUDÍ WAS GREATLY DE-VOTED TO THE VIRGIN MARY AND FOR THIS REASON HE DEDICATED THE APSE TOWER AND THE CHAPEL OF THE ASSUMPTION TO HER.

The series of constructions which make up the apse façade are comprised of four architectonic elements: the mentioned apse which rises up as a majestic backdrop, the chapel of the Assumption, the two sacristies located on the sides and the cloister, which unites the chapel with the sacristies. The cloister is included as one of the many innovations introduced by Gaudí into the Sagrada Familia with regards to traditional churches, given that instead of being set on one side it works as an element which unifies the numerous constructions which make up the Sagrada Familia monument. Where the cloister intersects with each façade there is a door dedicated to the Virgin. To show his successors how these doors should be decorated, Gaudí built the door dedicated to the Virgin of the Rosary, which he magnificently adorned with roses carved in stone, accompanied by sculptures and reliefs. The cult to the Virgin, was instituted as dogma by the Catholic Church from the time of Concilio de Trento (1545-1563) and reached its maximum splendour in the 19th century. Marian fervour echoed throughout the field of the arts, as many artists were dedicating their work to the veneration of the Virgin Mary. Antoni Gaudí was also greatly devoted to the Virgin, as demonstrated by his wish to be buried in the chapel dedicated to the Virgin Carmen, which is situated in the temple crypt. For this reason, he believed it was essential to devote a significant part of the temple to the maternal figure of the Holy Family.

Apse pinnacles. They are topped with representations of wheat ears and herbs.

Representation of some wild herbs

Jesus' anagram
Jesus' initial is surrounded by a crown of thorns, which is a symbol of his martyrdom.

Mary's anagram
The crown over Mary's initial symbolizes her condition as Queen of Heaven and Earth.

Work commences on the apse

Once the crypt was finished, work commenced on the apse, whose position over the former meant it repeated its structure. Gaudí, a fervent devotee to the Virgin, wanted to dedicate the apse to Mary. All the symbols and images adorning it are based on liturgical verses in allegiance to the Virgin, and the cimborio, which rises over the apse, is crowned by a large star, the *Stella matutina*, a classic Marian symbol. However, in the interior, the seven apse chapels commemorate the seven pains and pleasures of Saint Joseph, according to the wishes of its founder Bocabella, whose devotion to Saint Joseph gave rise to the temple.

Gaudí's passion for nature

Gaudí was a great observer of Nature. He had a deep admiration for all living beings and, in particular, plants and trees, which on numerous occasions were a source of inspiration in the aesthetic as well as technical sense. On one occasion he went so far as to say that his master was a tree which was growing near his workshop. Representations from the vegetable kingdom are frequent in his work, like the ears of wheat and floral motifs which top the pinnacles of the apse walls. Following this way of thinking, for the gargoyles on the apse, Gaudí preferred to use common animals traditionally related to evil. The amphibians and reptiles running down the walls are not allowed to enter the temple.

THE ANIMALS

Common animals on the apse
The gargoyles on the apse represent amphibians and reptiles, which are traditionally associated with evil.

Wall lizard

Earth snail

Frog

Lizard

● ● ●
THE DECORATION

Rose decoration
The explosion of roses which flood the portal come from the figure of the Virgin of the Rosary.

The death of the just man
The Virgin, accompanied by Joseph, shows the child Jesus to a suffering man who clasps a rosary in his hand.

● ● ●
PHOTOGRAPHS

❶ The portal is presided over by the Virgin with child. At their sides are Saint Domingo and Saint Catalina. ❷ **The temptation of Man.** Symbolic of violence, a demon offers an Orsini bomb to a worker. It was used by anarchists of the period. ❸ The walls are decorated with rosaries which are sculpted with great realism. ❹ Cloister vault keystone, sculpted with great precision.

The temple's innovative cloister
The function of the cloister, designed by Gaudí, was to unify the different areas and spaces of the Sagrada Familia. It encloses the temple within a 240 metre long rectangular extension, whose four sides correspond with the four façades. The Nativity, Glory and Passion portals break up its continuity. Four magnificent ornamental doorways were planned to maintain unity and to permit access through the façades. Meanwhile, the cloister is located at temple level and the difference in floor level with street level is taken advantage of by the construction of another floor.

The Rosary doorway
Each cloister intersection with a façade gives rise to a door dedicated to the Virgin. Those that are situated on both sides of the Nativity façade are dedicated to the Montserrat and Rosary Virgin. On the Passion façade, are the Virgin of Mercy and Our Lady of Sorrows. On the Rosary one, the cupola stands out illuminating all the doorway. All the architectonic elements, such as walls, vaults and arches, are decorated with a multitude of roses sculpted in stone with the precision of bobbin lace. The sculptor Etsuro Sotoo was in charge of sculpting in stone almost all of the sculptures on the portal, given that the original ones were destroyed in the Civil War.

● **THE CLOISTER.** Another of Gaudí's innovations was to recuperate the real significance
● of the cloister, which is meant to enclose. In monasteries and cathedrals, the cloister is
● located on one of the sides, but Gaudí's cloister surrounds the entire temple.

Life and the Nativity

TENDER AND JOYFUL, THIS FAÇADE DEPICTS THE MOST HUMAN SIDE OF JESUS. A GREAT CELEBRATION OF CREATION, IN WHICH ALL LIVING BEINGS REJOICE AT THE BIRTH OF THE MESSIAH.

The Nativity façade is also called *La Vida* (Life), *El Gozo* (Joy) and *La Navidad* (Christmas), given that it is an explosion of happiness on the birth of Jesus. The stone seems to lose its static appearance to convey the triumph of life with its own natural forms. This great stone nativity scene carries the message of Hope: The monument appears to herald: Jesus has been born, "Saviour of Mankind". Nature is shown in all its splendour and effervescence, as Christ's birth supposes the liberation of all life forms. On this spectacular façade, of World Heritage interest, the main events in Jesus' childhood and adolescence are depicted by means of sculptural groups: from the Annunciation up to his conversation in the Temple with the scholars about the Holy Scriptures, on to the flight to Egypt to his presentation in the Temple. The whole façade exudes a great tenderness, particularly in its portrayal of the most human and familiar facets of Jesus, such as when the adolescent worked alongside and assisted Saint Joseph in his carpentry workshop. To create a greater sensation of proximity and naivety, Gaudí turned to popular elements, such as domestic animals and tools, which the public could easily relate to. However, as with all of Gaudí's works, symbols of great complexity can also be found on this façade with which he sought to reach a higher transcendental plain.

**Inscription on
Jesus' column**

**Inscription on
Joseph's column**

**Inscription on
Mary's column**

**❶ The Nativity façade.
❷ Angels and trumpet-
ers.** With their bronze
trumpets, the angels
announce the birth of
Jesus. **❸ Turtle. ❹ The
cypress:** This tree sym-
bolises eternal life for its
resistant wood and its
evergreen leaves.

The Nativity façade

Gaudí wanted the Nativity façade to be the first one built to demonstrate all the plastic strength that could be achieved by the temple.
Work on the foundations commenced in February, 1894 and construction spanned the first third of the 20th century. Once the four
bell towers were finished in 1929 and the portal pinnacles completed
in 1932, there were only some sculptures left to be done, which were
then worked on over the years by various sculptors.

The columns that separate the porticos

The two big columns that are separating the porticos are of great
height and finely carved. On the base of each one there is a stone
turtle, which symbolizes the unalterable and never changes with
time. As for the shanks of the columns they are carved with upward-
ly spiralling grooves while the capitals are palm leaves from which
surge bunches of dates covered in snow, acting as support to the
four angel trumpeters who announce the Birth of the Baby Jesus to
the four winds.

● **THE THREE PORTICOS.** The Nativity façade is comprised of three porticos and four
● bell towers. The porticos are dedicated to three theological virtues, which are each
● related to a member of the Holy Family. The central portico, the highest of all, is dedicated to Charity, whose maximum exponent is Jesus. The portico on the right-hand side
is dedicated to Faith and devoted to Mary. Lastly, the portico on the left is that of Hope,
whose best exponent was Saint Joseph.

Gloria in excelsis Deo...
Inscribed in Latin on the upper part of the doors is, *"Glory to God on high and on earth peace to all men of goodwill"*, which is the phrase the angels said to the shepherds on the announcement of the birth of Jesus.

The Charity portico

The central portico, which is also called Love, is the largest on the façade. Built as if it were an enormous cave, within it are the characters that were present at the Birth of Jesus. On the lower part of the Charity Portico is a column of spiral form, which is carved in relief and details the family tree of Jesus. This pillar supports the Holy Family, which is represented in the sculptural group on the Nativity. The recently born Jesus protected by Joseph and Mary rests on the column capital. Completing this scene, are also the ox and mule, symbolic of the Messiah's humbleness. All the sculptural and architectonic elements of the façade are arranged so that the viewer's attention is focused on the baby Jesus figure.

The adoration of the shepherds and the Kings

The shepherds and the animals look on at the newly born Jesus with great tenderness, moved by having found the son of God. They were the first to see the star of Bethlehem and to worship the Baby Jesus. They

Sculptural group of the Nativity. Work by sculptor Joan Busquets.

The star of Bethlehem

The gift from the shepherds

symbolize the people. As well, Melchior, Caspar and Balthazar, the Three Wise Men from the Orient and guided by the Star of Bethlehem, introduced themselves to Jesus with offerings of gold, frankincense and myrrh.

The Coronation of Mary

Topping the portico, this amazing work by Joan Matamala, according to Gaudí's project, depicts the moment when the Virgin was crowned as reward for her self-sacrificing love to God.

The Annunciation of Mary

The sculptural group, situated between the groups of the Coronation of Mary and the angel musicians, shows the moment in which the archangel Gabriel informs a submissive and devoted Mary, that she has been chosen to be the Mother of the Son of God. The scene is completed with a rosary and numerous birds breaking out of the stone.

The dog
As well as a popular illustration, it symbolises loyalty.

Domestic animals
As in a nativity scene, the pedestals of the Adoration of the Shepherds and the Three Wise Men are covered with a large variety of birds and plants.

● **THE CHORUS OF BABY ANGELS.** The original sculptures were made of plaster and
● were destroyed during the Civil War. Those that can now be seen are an interpretation by
● sculptor Etsuro Sotoo, based on the ideas that Antoni Gaudí left behind.

The birds
With dynamism, groups of birds emanate from the stone.

The Hope portico. With this portico Gaudí reunited the childhood situations of Jesus which better embody Joseph and his virtue, hope. ❶ **The Massacre of the Innocents.** With great dramatic force, this event is presented by a soldier of enormous dimensions who on the point of killing a new born baby is unperturbed by the pleading cries of its mother. ❷ **Saint Joseph's boat.** Saint Joseph appears as the helmsman who led the Catholic church, which is symbolized by the boat. The figure of Saint Joseph looks very much like Gaudí, given that, supposedly, it was the tribute which the temple workers paid to him after his death. ❸ **The flight to Egypt.** The Holy Family fled to Egypt to avoid the death of Jesus at the hands of Herod's soldiers. An angel, energetically pulls on the ass which is ridden by the

Virgin with the baby in her arms. **❹ Tools.** Gaudí combined the holy (the rosary) with the everyday, personified by the great variety of tools sculpted.

The Faith portico. This portico is dedicated to the Faith and the Virgin Mary who is maximum exponent of this virtue. Some of the most significant scenes from Jesus' childhood and adolescence in the Gospel are depicted here. **❺ The Visitation.** The Virgin Mary visits her cousin Elisabeth to tell her that she is expecting the Messiah. **❻ Jesus working.** Situated on the right-hand side of the portico, this sculpture of great realism represents a young Jesus aiding Joseph in his carpentry workshop in Nazareth.

Death and the Passion

SPARSE DECORATION WITH SCULPTURES OF HARD SCHEMATIC FORMS, THIS FAÇADE CONVEYS CHRIST'S SUFFERING DURING THE LAST DAYS OF HIS LIFE.

When observing the Passion façade, a certain perception of coldness and sadness is unavoidable. For this is what it strives to achieve, to show the suffering or the Passion of Christ and his death. Gaudí was conscious of the impact that this portal would have on the citizens, which was why he decided to start its construction once the Nativity façade had been completed. By doing so, he avoided popular rejection and gained more leeway in order that the global message of the temple would be understood. To convey this idea of desolation and pain, Gaudí freed the façade from any type of ornamentation. Likewise, he simplified its structure leaving clean hard bone-like shapes, with no more adornment than the cold nudity of the stone. The reason for this absence of decoration is so that attention is primarily paid to the groups of sculptures that describe the last days in the life of Jesus. The whole portal functions as an enormous stage where the most relevant events in the Passion of Jesus Christ unfold in chronological order before the viewer's eyes. Responsible for the execution of the sculptures on this façade is Josep Maria Subirachs. This Catalan sculptor has interpreted the material that Gaudí left behind imprinting, on the façade's sculptures, an austere and nude line. His work is characterised by its angled and schematic forms, whose marked profiles help to underline the drama of the monument.

●●●

SCULPTURES

The kiss of Judas
Sealing his betrayal, Judas kisses Jesus to indicate whom his master is to the soldiers who lie in wait, awaiting the signal to arrest him. This scene took place at night, on the Mount of Olives.

Peter and his denial
Peter denied knowing his master on three occasions; his posture and facial expression reflect the shame he feels for his actions. As a metaphor of his denial, the apostle appears swathed in a sheet and three women represent his three denials.

●●●

PHOTOGRAPHS

**❶ The Last Supper.
❷ The serpent. ❸ The cryptogram.** Consists of a square containing 16 numbers. The sum of these, in 310 different combinations, always adds up to 33, Christ's age when he died. **❹ The dog.**

The Passion according to Gaudí

In 1911, Gaudí withdrew to Puigcerdà to recuperate from a serious illness which was life-threatening. He was inspired by his own suffering and he set upon planning the Passion façade, where he wanted to imprint all the hardness of sacrifice. Gaudí left behind various drawings, studies and sketches on how the structure and decoration should be.

It was in 1954 that work commenced on the façade according to Gaudí's project, which consisted of a portico supported by six leaning columns, over which a great frontage is sustained by 18 small bone-shaped columns. This frontage is the last thing remaining to be built on all of the Passion façade monument.

Subirachs, the sculptor

In 1986, Josep Maria Subirachs was commissioned to work on the sculptural groups on the façade. After dedicating a year's study to Gaudí's work, Subirachs started sculpting in 1987 and from this moment, just like Gaudí, has been fully dedicated to what has become the most important work of his life. As his sculptures show, Subirachs is defined as an extremely cerebral sculptor.

● **THE PASSION FAÇADE.** In contrast to the optimism and vitality exuded by the decorative
● exuberance of the Nativity façade, the Passion façade expresses the pain and anguish of
● Jesus Christ's death with austerity and harshness. West-facing, where the sun sets every day, this façade recalls the cruelty of sacrifice by means of a series of sculptural groups that represent the last days in the life of Jesus up until his death.

● **THE GOSPEL DOORS.** Over the central door the gospel text is reproduced and narrates what the façade sculptures illustrate, the
● last two days of Jesus. This way, the doors function like the pages of a monumental New Testament. 8,000 bronze characters were
● cast to write the text on the Gospel doors. Some words of particular significance are polished so that they stand out from the rest.

**The Coronation of
Thorns door**
Jesus facing Pilate.

The Gethsemane door
The disciples sleep.

The three Doors

The central doors, those of the Gospel, synthetically symbolize the work on the façade, explaining in words what the different sculptural groups illustrate.

On them the Gospel text is reproduced, narrating the last two days in the life of Jesus. This way, the doors, separated by a mullion, function as the pages of a monumental New Testament, which serves as a backdrop to the flagellation figure.

The Gethsemane door, located on the façade's left-hand side, measures 5.87 metres high and 2.40 metres wide. It is made of bronze and was carried out between 1992 and 1994. The reliefs depict Jesus praying in the garden while three of his disciples are asleep. Verses describing this scene are also written.

Finally, on the right of the façade is the Coronation of Thorns door, where the central relief depicts the humiliation that Jesus suffered at the hands of the Roman soldiers when after his torture; they gave him a crown of thorns and a cane as a sceptre. In the middle part is shown, like a mirror effect, the presentation of Jesus before Herod, on the left-hand side, and before Pilate, on the right. On the door's surface a quotation from Dante's *Divine Comedy* is engraved along with some verses from a poem by Salvador Espriu.

THE FLAGELLATION

This event is one of the most dramatic moments of the Passion of Christ, given that Jesus is completely alone during his flagellation. Not one of his disciples or his family are there, with only his torturers surrounding him. To convey with greater vehemence this terrible feeling of solitude, the sculpture has been placed between the denial of Peter and the betrayal of Judas. It is the most important figure on the lower level, reaching a height of five metres and is sculpted in travertine marble of the highest quality. Around the sculpture are the instruments that were used during his torture.

The knot. Sculpted with great realism, the knot symbolizes the physical torture suffered by Christ.

The cane. It symbolizes psychological torture. It reflects the ridicule that Christ suffered when the soldiers gave him a cane instead of a mitre, a sign of royalty.

The Holy Spirit. Is represented by an abstract dove, the classic symbol of the Holy Spirit.

The Lamb. Done in brightly coloured ceramic work, it symbolizes the resurrection of Jesus.

The burial. Joseph of Arimatea and Nicodemus put the body of Jesus, which is wrapped in a sheet, into the tomb. Mary kneels down at the tomb entrance. The cracks on the wall symbolize the fulfilment of the Scriptures and the earthquake on Christ's death. ❶

The crucifixión. Jesus has now died on the cross. On his left are Mary Magdalene, kneeling, and the Virgin Mary, who is being consoled by John. A little further back is Mary of Cleophas. The cross is made with two iron bars. The front part of the start of the vertical bar is painted the colour red to highlight an "I", the first letter of the inscription I.N.R.I. ❷

The Ascension of Christ. The façade is crowned by a bronze sculpture measuring 5 metres and weighing 2000 kilos. ❸

The "Veronica" and the evangelist. Shows Jesus' second falter on the Calvary path. In the middle of the scene Veronica appears showing the veil on which Jesus' face is marked. Her figure has no face in order that more attention is paid to Jesus' face. Here, the sculptor, pays homage to Gaudí: by the evangelist and soldiers' helmets, which represent Casa Milà's chimneys. This sculptural group is the most numerous on the façade, as it is made up of seventeen figures. ❹

The three Marys, Simon of Cyrene and Jesus lying on the floor

The soldier Longinus and his horse

Gaudí's towers

BY ENDOWING THE TEMPLE EXTERIOR WITH A GREAT
HEIGHT GAUDÍ ENSURED THAT IT WOULD BE
THE MOST STRIKING CONSTRUCTION IN THE CITY.

In any period or civilization, religious constructions have striven to differentiate themselves from other buildings by their shape and, above all, by their dimensions. Height bestows prestige and dignity upon a building that is itself a mystic symbol, representing the union of man with God. For this reason, Antoni Gaudí wanted his temple to be higher than any other building in Barcelona and its exterior was endowed with extraordinary dimensions. This monument is made up of eighteen towers whose heights are determined according to their religious hierarchy and the symbolic message that they represent. Therefore, the central cimborio, the highest and most important, is the one that represents Jesus Christ and measures 170 metres high and is crowned with a 15 metre high cross. Surrounding his cimborio are four towers dedicated to the four evangelists, measuring 125 metres high, while the cimborio that is devoted to the Virgin Mary reaches 120 metres and soars over the apse. Lastly, in order of height the twelve bell towers that represent the apostles serve as backdrop to the three façades. Their parabolic profile, like enormous needles piercing and cutting through the city skyline, make the bell towers the most characteristic element of the temple. When all of the towers are erected, the Sagrada Familia will majestically surpass any other Christian church built by Man.

THE DETAILS

The phrases
On the bell towers, the word *Sanctus* is repeated and decorated in colour ceramic work. Each group of three *Sanctus* is dedicated to the Father, the Son and the Holy Spirit. Also carved in stone palm leaves are the names of the Holy Family and the expression *Sursum Corda* that in Latin stands for *lift up your hearts*.

Bosses
Close-up of one of the 12 bosses that decorate each bell tower.

A symbol of Barcelona

The exterior of the monument holds an extraordinary symbolism, which Gaudí knew how to give expression to with four models of towers. The four rising from the three façades represent the twelve apostles. Over the temple is situated the highest tower, which symbolizes Jesus. This is surrounded by four cimborios which are dedicated to the evangelists. Lastly, the apse is covered by a large tower dedicated to Mary. Gaudí wanted the towers of Sagrada Familia to be higher than any other civil building in the city to demonstrate the supremacy of the divine over the human. The temple had to be the urban landscape's reference point and, therefore be visible from all corners of Barcelona. With this objective in mind, the central cimborio was planned, dedicated to Jesus, measuring 170 metres high, just a few metres less than that of the nearby mountain of Montjuïc. By way of surrendering to Nature, the architect upheld his belief that Man can't outdo what God has created.

Gaudí's inspiration

The originality of the work of Antoni Gaudí surged from his imagination, but also stemmed from his penetrating and analytical observation of reality. He himself recognised that a great part of his merit stemmed from his capacity to observe what tends to go unnoticed by others. The singular conical shape of the towers has been compared with three very different realities: the human towers made by the "*castellers*", the north African mosques and the geological formations in the Valley of the Fairies in Turkey.

VIEW FROM THE MOUNTAIN. Due to their great height, the towers of the Sagrada Familia stand out from the rest of the buildings and, like a lighthouse, it can be seen from different points in the city. Its silhouette has become a symbol of the city of Barcelona.

The bell towers. Are located on the Nativity, Passion and Glory façade and represent Jesus' twelve apostles. Gaudí thought of two complex solutions for the twelve bell tower endings. The first one consisted of a look-out tower with a hexagonal base and pyramidal shape with rings. The second proposal, which was the one chosen in the end and carried out, meant that each tower was topped with a pinnacle decorated with Venetian polychromatic mosaic work and crowned with a double-sided shield, a cross and white spheres, in reference to the Episcopal mitre. **❶ ❷ ❸**

The pinnacles. Measuring 25 metres high, the tower pinnacles stand out from the rest of the bell towers for their complex shape and rich coloured mosaic patterns they are

covered with. This variety of shape, colour and material means, as well as a spectacular aesthetic effect, that the pinnacles are visible from far away. Gaudí used these decorative elements to unite the four symbols that represent bishops: the mitre, cross, staff and ring. The reason for which these Episcopal symbols are represented on the peak of the bell towers is that the bishops are responsible for carrying on the evangelical work of the first apostles.

The apostles. Each bell tower carries the name and sculpture of the apostle that it represents; **Barnabus ❹, Matthias, Simon and Judas** are on the Nativity façade, while **Thomas ❺, James the Lesser, Philip and Bartholomew** are on the Passion façade.

The temple interior

THE ESSENCE OF GAUDÍ'S ARCHITECTURE IS CONCENTRATED WITHIN THE SAGRADA FAMILIA: ITS COLUMN AND VAULT SYSTEM HAS NO EQUIVALENT IN THE HISTORY OF ARCHITECTURE.

The Latin cross ground plan is the only concession that Gaudí made to classical structures in the temple interior. The rest of the architectonic elements of which it is comprised are, as most of Gaudí's work, totally original. The solution for the temple naves was subject to an in-depth study and much consideration, which led to three different projects until a totally innovative architectonic solution was found. The first project, presented in 1898, was basically Gothic, although the need for buttresses had been corrected. Due to a detailed study of weights, Gaudí managed to transfer pressure from the vaults directly to the floor by using extremely canted arches. Nevertheless, this project didn't fully satisfy the architect for two reasons: the temple continued being, in essence, Gothic and each arch mechanically depended on the adjoining one, so if one failed, it would drag the other one down in its fall. It was then at the age of 70 that Gaudí found the solution he so yearned for, in the use of arborescent columns. These columns, tilting and branching out like a tree, meant buttresses could be avoided, as the weight of the roof would be directed to the floor thus freeing the outer walls. This ingenious architectural system has, likewise, a spectacular aesthetic consequence, as the temple interior is transformed into an enormous stone forest, where light harmoniously filters through its vaults and outer walls.

Wall. A gallery goes around the interior walls of the temple.

Nativity façade interior; 1894 to 1930

Tears. Located in the inside part of the Nativity façade.

The stones. Gaudí positioned blocks of stone of basic shape to be sculpted later on.

Symbology inside the temple

Inside the temple the four daily prayers are represented, just like the Gospels and epistles that are read out in Sunday mass. To illuminate the area where liturgy takes place, there will be a lamp with seven arms symbolizing the Holy Spirit. As in all Christian temples, the main altar will be presided over by a cross, from which will surge a vine whose tendrils and grapes will form the baldachin that covers it. To complete the Holy Trinity, the apse tower will be covered with mosaic work and the vestments of God will be symbolized on its celestial vault.

A temple of huge dimensions

The temple has a Latin cross ground plan and is made up of five longitudinal naves, with a transept measuring 60 metres long by 45 metres wide. The total length, from the entrance to the apse, is 90 metres. The central nave is 15 metres wide with the lateral ones measuring half : 7.5m. The central nave vaults reach a height of 45 metres, while the lateral nave ones reach 30 metres.

The vaults situated below the central cimborio reach 60 metres and those of the apse soar to 75. With these dimensions, the Sagrada Familia will be one of the largest temples in the world.

THE VAULTS...

In contrast to former cathedrals, whose vaults were robust and had to support a lot of weight, Gaudí wanted Sagrada Familia's vaults to be light-weight and illuminate the temple interior. The vaults emerge from tree-like columns and form palm leaves which represent the symbol of martyrdom. The assembly point of the leaves, some concave and others convex, also allow the filtering of light into the temple.

...& THE COLUMNS

During many years of study, Gaudí wanted the temple columns to be as robust and beautiful as the trees in a forest. The architect fled from vertical rigidity by tilting and turning them in spiral form to simulate how a tree trunk grows. Likewise, when they reached a certain height, the columns divided out into branchlike form to increase the number of support elements and to better distribute the weight of the roofs and the vaults. This arborescent design allowed Gaudí to optimise the different loads and to be able to lessen the diameter of all the columns.

● ● ●

THE ENDINGS

Grapes and wine
The terminations of the various pinnacles of the central nave, carried out by Etsuro Sotoo, are used to exhibit the grapes and wine as symbol of the Eucharist.

The fruit. The sculptor Etsuro Sotoo also did the endings on the lateral façade pinnacles, which consist of baskets of fruit: apples, figs, peaches, loquats, pomegranates and cherries.

● ● ●

PHOTOGRAPH

Joan Vila-Grau, has been working on the temple's stained glass windows since 1999, interpreting the chromatic concept devised by Gaudí. Thus, the lower windows will be of an intense colour, the higher ones of a lighter colour and those on the upper floor will be done in a combination of colourless glass of varying texture.

The windows and the lateral walls

Thanks to the ingenious arborescent system that Gaudí used in the temple interior, the lateral walls are freed from supporting the roof weight. In contrast to other styles, like the Romanic or Gothic styles, Gaudí's lateral façades only have to support their own structure, meaning they can be much lighter. One of the main consequences of this greater lightness is that it provides more liberty when opening up spaces for the entrance of natural light. Therefore, all the walls are dotted with numerous windows of various shape and size by which the temple's naves are harmoniously illuminated.

The temple of light

The windows, the vaults and, in general, all the sources of light were designed to illuminate the temple interior the same way as light filters through the leaves in a forest. Gaudí pursued a harmonious indirect illumination, which highlighted the plasticity of the architecture, while at the same time showed off the temple's decoration and transmitted a feeling of spiritual peace.

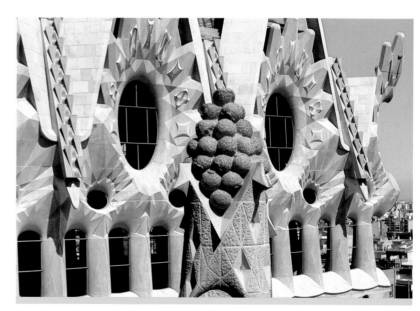

● **THE WALLS AND THE WINDOWS.** As the nave lateral walls only support their own
● weight, it is possible to put in many large windows, which allow a better illumination of
● the temple allowing the sun light to gently filter through.

The schoolrooms

THE SCHOOLROOMS ARE A MAGNIFICENT EXAMPLE OF GAUDÍ'S CAPACITY TO TRANSFORM A HUMBLE MATERIAL INTO A CONSTRUCTION THAT IS AS SURPRISING AS IT IS TECHNICALLY IMPECCABLE.

Despite its small dimensions, the building that housed the provisional schoolrooms is considered as one of the most representative of Gaudí's works, given that simplicity, functionality and innovation are combined within. The Association of Devotees to Saint Joseph, promoters of the temple, along with the Father Gil Parés, chaplain of Sagrada Familia, paid great importance to primary and secondary education. For this reason it was Gil Parés who commissioned Gaudí to construct a small building that would serve as an educational centre for the children of the workers participating in the construction on the temple and for the children in the neighbourhood. The architect responded by constructing an extremely economical and practical building. Built with Catalan brick, which wasn't rendered over, Gaudí divided the interior of the building by means of two walls, giving rise to three classrooms. Moreover, the architect used three metallic pillars to support the master beam on which the roof beams rested. Undoubtedly, the structure's conodial cover is the most surprising and distinctive element of the building. The innovative spirit of the work perfectly identified with the pedagogical system used in education. The religious Gil Parés' views on education were very progressive for the period as he believed in the active school, where practical and instructive knowledge prevailed. The schoolrooms were in use from 1909 until the late eighties, when the lack of students led to its closure as educational centre.

Change of location
The need to change the position of the schools couldn't be put off any more as their location prevented work progressing on the temple. In order that the transferred building was as faithful as possible to the original, Gaudí's construction method was studied and a copy was even built. The elements that were preserved the best were transferred whole and each piece was put into its respective place, integrating the recovered materials with the new ones.

Gaudí's table
The schoolroom's museum has a copy of Gaudí's work table.

● ● ●

PHOTOGRAPHS

❶ A lamp over the entrance. ❷ Close up of the windows. ❸ One of the move's objectives was to recuperate the original appearance of Gaudí's building, lost after its reconstruction in 1936.

A rational and simple construction

The schoolrooms were built between 1908 and 1909 and functioned as a teaching centre for more than 70 years. Their external appearance is of great simplicity as they would be demolished as soon as more space was needed in the temple grounds and Gaudí also wanted minimal cost. The most distinctive feature of the building is its undulating roof and walls. The sinuous form provides the structure with a great resistance in a simple and rational way. In July 1936, shortly after the start of the Spanish Civil War, an uncontrolled group of people set fire to the schoolrooms. The fire badly affected the building and its roof collapsed. The architect F. Quintana took charge of its reconstruction introducing various modifications to Gaudí's building.

Gaudí's workshop

At present, the schoolrooms house the didactic room of the Sagrada Familia museum. Amongst other curiosities, there is a replica of Gaudí's work table, given that the original was in his studio near the apse, and the work table is where he would lay out his plans and plaster cast models. Models of the Glory façade, the sacristies and the columns can also be viewed.

● **THE SCHOOLROOMS.** In one of the corners of the Sagrada Familia grounds are the
● schoolrooms that Gaudí designed and constructed for the labourers' children and fami-
● lies in the neighbourhood. The simplicity of this construction is only apparent, given that, as with all of the architect's works, its exterior reflects great aesthetic originality, while its structure is a clear example of innovative technical solutions.